I. Introduction Surviving

The fu*k! What the fu*k do you want?! I mean, I cook, clean, work, look pretty, worry in silence, smile, laugh, problem-solve, and stretch money like a bikini thong.... So please, tell me what else could you possibly want?

It seems we can't catch a break huh ladies... It is my hope that not only single mothers but also fathers and everyone connected to us will read this book and gain some valuable insight to the life that we live.

P.S. sometimes good moms 'cuss a little. Wink wink.

IN THE BEGINNING, I WAS PREGNANT

I remember my first pregnancy very clearly. I thought I was just gaining weight at first. Fresh and home off a mental breakdown I had at college, I was exhausted from working and going to school full time, with no outside support except a little here and there; it proved to be too much. I was at my girlfriend's house when I was introduced—or as we used to say back then, "set up"—with this guy. After he and I started spending more time together, we had sex, only once, which was also only the second time that I had ever done "the nasty" in my 22 years of life. Life was normal and calm, then I started gaining weight. I'm thinking, dang, I must be eating good. I began working out, then came the nausea and vomiting. After about a week of that, I went to the doctor, and they tested me for the flu, pregnancy, and everything else they could think of with these symptoms. All of the tests came back clear; I was given a clean bill of health and sent home, and yes, the pregnancy test was negative, THANK GOD. 24 hours later, the nurse called me to come back; they wanted to draw blood. I'm confused, what's this for? Lord, please don't tell me I have an STD! They sent me home again. 2 days later, I got a call saying the results show I'm pregnant? Wait, What??? Apparently, my body's HCG levels weren't high enough to show on the pee stick tests that most of us take, so surprise! I'm devastated; I want to go back to school, not raise a baby.

I'm living in my late grandparents' house, working a minimum wage job. I literally threw up all day every day, eventually losing my job because you can't throw up and work around food. Yeah, no, I can't possibly do this, not a baby. I went to my aunt, my mother's older sister, and asked her if I wanted to get an abortion if she would go with me? She said yes, but that she wouldn't give an opinion on it because the decision had to be solely mine. I set the appointment and, on that day, walked to her house, and we set out towards the clinic. On the way there, as we drove, I couldn't breathe; I asked her very hastily to pull over. She never asked why; she simply pulled off to the side. I sat there crying and finally said I couldn't do it; I couldn't get rid of the baby. She calmly got out of the car and went to the trunk. I had no idea what she was going to do, but the trunk? She returned inside the car with the biggest smile, holding up a bunch of baby stuff she had already bought for my baby. The relief of knowing someone was in my corner was overwhelming. That was baby number one, who would ultimately become one of six births, five that are alive. I'll tell you about the other four in another book. LOL This single mother stuff is crazy, and no, contrary to what stereotypes would have you believe, it isn't planned. Nor is it some kind of punishment from God. Your life isn't over (yet); one day it will be for sure, just a little realism, but for today, we fight on.

> "Some days I wonder if my kids will remember the mom who baked, cuddled, and loved them…. or the overstimulated psycho."

This book is the space where single mothers can breathe without judgement, let our hair down, feel, grow, connect. There are so many times when we hold in our emotions and opinions, good and bad, for the benefit and welfare of others. We rarely get a chance to defend ourselves without someone turning it around to make us look bitter and off balance. We will explore these emotions, address the myths and vent, when and however we feel. Many say how do you define a single mother? I'm glad you asked…. A single mother is, by definition, an unmarried mother that doesn't have a live-in spouse or partner to help in the upbringing or support of their child. The keyword here= LIVE-IN.

Chapter 1: The Unseen Struggles

WHOA, BABY!

So, let's start at the beginning when it was fun. We flirted, dated, and of course, we had sex. (Well, obviously.) Girl, look at him. I bet you are standing there seeing him, thinking, "What in the world was I thinking?" Just look at him. Now you can't find anything attractive—not his hair, his body. Now you realize his teeth are crooked too. You had sex with that average body and an even more averaged size dick-having, mean-ass, beer belly, ashy-ass man?

Okay, okay, calm down. Maybe the D was big and felt really good... Haha, in that case, I know EXACTLY why you did it! Whew, chile. Alright, now settle down and don't you dare pick up that phone! Snap out of it, sis. Put the phone down! Don't you dare call him. I'm not trying to send any of y'all backward.

Let's fast forward a few weeks, and BAM, you're late. Or are you? Wait, when did my last period start? Dang, yeah, you're definitely late. Oh boy, let me go get a pregnancy test or three; the first one could be wrong. This is the longest few minutes of my life, time's up! Two lines! Omg, I'm pregnant! Sigh…Now, to tell him or not to tell him? That is the question. Hmm, if you love him, yes, you automatically tell him but probably make a big fuss of it, though you still worry about what his reaction will be. If you don't love or like him, you worry about whether or not you want to be bothered with his sh*t for the next eighteen years and how you will manage as a single mother. How will everyone else react? Parents, friends, grandmomma nem'? Should I have an abortion or keep the baby? And then again, there's always adoption. Can I even afford it? If I want to have an abortion, could I really go through with it? Will I have to go alone? What if someone finds out? If I give the baby up for adoption, will they grow up to be mad at me? Feel unloved? Go to a good home? Will I be able to see them later? Grrr... What to do?!

I'm unsure about how everyone will react, but I'm actually not sad at all, surprised maybe, definitely not sad. However, this could be great! I love the little bundle already; I wonder if it's a boy or girl? What name will I choose depending on the sex? Hmm, now back to the first question, what to do?

I've made up my mind; I'm keeping this baby, and I don't care what anyone has to say. I will love and take care of this baby by myself if I have to. That isn't my first choice; Lord, please make it alright. Please. Doctors' appointments are always exciting, finding out how far along you are and watching your baby grow. Prenatal pills suck! Yuck. Morning sickness that sometimes lasts all day and weird cravings are so random, but yes, your body is changing, and you still want to feel beautiful. Feeling comfortable is your life right now; you're embracing the changes and more than likely feeling stuff that ain't really there, ha-ha.

I've told everyone, and though some might not like it, they are embracing the news. When/if my family turns their backs on me, then thank God for my friends and vice versa; having both is a total life hack. Going to church every Sunday is a little sticky because I know everyone is getting ready to judge me like they've never done anything except live holy, but for now, I'm not showing much. I'm praying for strength and guidance as I go on this journey!

I've made it to the second trimester, and beginning to show, I can't wait to find out the sex of the baby. How exciting! By this time, maybe you and the father of the baby are back together; maybe y'all are considering marriage, maybe he's not claiming the baby at all, and either way, you keep preparing, buying, decorating, "nesting" to prepare for the baby's arrival.

The folks who love and support you have gotten together and thrown you an awesome baby shower. By now, all the speculating and rumors of your pregnancy have hopefully started to die down. It's always surprising to me how much time and effort people invest in trying to determine the identity of the father, how many other kids you have, whether you're together or not, along with speculating on any other gossip they can come up with that's not their business. This entire pregnancy, you have been working, paying bills, and still being there for everybody else. Fighting through body discomfort is hard, especially if you don't live with someone that can help comfort you. You may lie alone, rubbing your tummy and feeling sad sometimes, and more than likely, tired and cranky too. Wearing that tough exterior can be heavy, no one that I know wants to go thru pregnancy alone, it brings a different type of sadness. One positive thing is that you're kind of cute with your big belly; you've let sexy go but are still very proud of your baby bump. Keep your hands off my belly! I'm not a puppy; don't pet me, grown people thinking pregnancy gives you a hall pass to the unwanted touching of strangers is crazy.

The funniest part might be all the peeing, eat, pee, walk five steps, pee, sleep, pee, stand or sit, pee. LOL

The room is done now, and if you could just walk that baby out! Here you are googling ways to induce labor; all the while the baby's foot is stuck under your rib cage, which often makes you look funny to other folks who don't know you're shifting to get the baby to change position. I bet people-watching pregnant women is a hilarious sight! Ouch, ahhh, whew, ahhh, I think I'm in labor, wait nah, I'm tripping.. No, no, ouch, ahh ok that's definitely pain, I'M IN LABOR! Off to the hospital we go!

Delivery was hard but so worth it, thank goodness for those labor and delivery nurses that started telling us we are almost there from the very first moment we start pushing. No complications, finally, baby and mom are home. Even when things don't go as we humans plan and our baby enters the world with little imperfections, all we mothers see is perfection, sweet music to our ears. New babies bring lots of fresh help in the beginning; hopefully, you have a support system and even then, you're glad for the occasional visitor just to be able to take a shower without being paranoid. We start out with all these germophobic tendencies, but that quickly wears off. Your husband, boyfriend, ex, slash soon-to-be baby's daddy (you're probably wondering how I know this, but if you're a single mother, then, well) …. is spending longer and longer in the bathroom, work, store, and anywhere else it seems, other than where and when you need his help with itty-bitty. You two have been arguing and fighting, now you're just plain old tired, tired of wanting better, tired of fussing, physically tired, just drained.

Trust me when I say if one of you is unhappy, more likely than not, the other person is too. Eventually, y'all break up, and now he's out here living like he's single, sexy, and free. Meanwhile, you're over here run down tired. Isn't it amazing how most, I won't say all of us mothers, give up our hottest years to the wrong man? Only to watch him go find some young pop tart with the body we used to have. Flat stomachs, narrow feet and noses, no extra hips and thighs nor anything else we would've said eww to in our early twenties.

We lay down with, marry and date these men who fill us with life literally, then walk away after draining us mentally, physically and emotionally. Ain't that a b*tch. Unpacking the reasons we choose the type of man we choose is a whole nother book. Just because y'all don't work as a couple doesn't mean he isn't a good father, him not fathering is what makes him suck as a father. When men get back into the dating scene, the way they maneuver is so different from that of single mothers because for the most part it's not changed, that is unless they physically have the kids with them for the day or weekend.

It took some time for society to begin embracing the post-pregnancy body. I'm glad we are finally getting our shine. This may seem purely surface-level conversation on the viewpoint but take a moment to think about when you're around a group of women, there's rarely an occasion where one of them isn't talking about trying to lose weight or get their body back. Hopefully, you have some friends that'll come hang or take you out from time to time; they may even tell you to comb your hair, nah… I'm just playing; most of us still be looking fly after the first baby anyway. Going back to work and leaving your brand-new baby with stranger's sucks balls, giant ones! No matter how nice, clean and warm the daycare is, it doesn't make it any easier. Having a family that'll help is a Godsend; go to work, pick up baby, dinner, clean and sleep is always the plan; if you don't execute it flawlessly, oh well, sh*t's exhausting, but worth that smile from the babies when they see you at the end of the day.

Dear Diary,
Today I am choosing violence. Not sure when, where, or even why. But, today feels like the right day.

Chapter 2: Embracing Independence and Resilience

TIRED OF THE SH*T

So now that you know the backstory, let's get to the nitty-gritty for all of you punk-a** married women who are so lonely and unhappy in your single mom married life that you try to look down on us single moms. I said what I said. YES, we can clearly see that you're married, but we can also clearly see that you are doing everything *ALONE*.

First off, no need to let *us* know you're married with that lame "someone else's husband ain't your soulmate" post. Maybe you should <u>remind your man</u> so that he can stay out of single women's inboxes. OOPS. See, nobody wants to address the single women that have been lied to by UN-single men. Nobody wants to address women getting into relationships that are complicated because they still want to believe and have hope that love still exists for them, even when it seems like a long shot. This can be a cruel cold a** world we live in, there aren't many that can survive in it alone. Nobody wants to discuss the systems put in place to keep families fighting rather than united.

    Single moms have to deal with their *own sh*t* their *employers' sh*t*, their *kids' sh*t* and *your sh*t* too. But we are supposed to be or appear to be happy all the time? And those little broke besties (kids) we got; we love 'em but they are sickening as hell sometimes. I was so happy when the only private part I had to see, clean, and dress was my own. I now look forward to my early morning coffee before they wake up, in peace and quiet, and after bedtime, where I can unwind from the day and possibly watch a show uninterrupted until I fall asleep, that is. Those nights when they are sick, and we stay up worried, and nursing the fever until it's down, cleaning throw-up, rocking them all night long in a chair, rubbing their pain until it goes away, these are the things you tend to feel better about in hindsight because in the moment you're so worn out that you just want it to be over.

    Not to mention that after a long night awake with a sick child, you're going to have to drag your butt into work the next morning, where undoubtedly people will judge your mood based on how you look and whether or not you're chatty or smiling. This is the space where I pause and say yes, being a single mom makes you special, not because you had sex and got pregnant with a "I don't want to be a daddy" baby daddy... pause... Yes, read that again.

You are special because you are doing what needs to be done in spite of.

In spite of judging your own choices that led you here

In spite of your lack of resources

In spite of judgment from the church, family, and friends

In spite of those who hope you fail

In spite of people trying to scandalize your name

In spite of you not knowing what the right thing to do is sometimes.

You still show up every day, all day, 365 days a year. Are there days when you want to quit? HELL YEAH! Are there days when you think that you will break under the pressure? HELL YEAH. Thoughts of suicide, abandonment, signing them over to another family member? Quite possibly. Those thoughts and feelings are natural. Stress, depression, anguish, fear all have their moments; however, we can't let the dark days win. It is unnatural to wear these feelings until you don't know life without them.

LISTEN... this is a hard one, ladies, very hard. The best thing to do for your kids might be to let someone else who loves them take care of them. Many of you may be thinking NEVER, as am I, but another mother may be in a space where she needs to in order to protect and take care of them; and there ain't no shame in that.

GUT CHECK YOURSELF

Sometimes moms fail, we do y'all. There are times when we drop the ball; all kids aren't living in bliss, and there are things we know we could do better, but I'm not talking about that. I'm talking about those who know they are doing wrong by their kids and choose to continue rather than changing. Oftentimes, we hear the stories when they are older as adults sharing their experiences about the hell they've lived thru; most of times these are things the whole neighborhood could see while they were growing up, but folks chose to stay out of it. We have to remember they were once young, and had some changes been made back then, they would be better off now.

Check yourself before you wreck yourself comes to mind. Beating yourself up for what you don't know is senseless; there are so many resources available to you via the internet, schools, and community organizations. Adults need mentors too. That is a complete sentence all by itself. You keep growing, and your kids will too. I know how it feels to hide your emotions from your children when you're sad, crying in the shower or while you lay in bed alone at night. Pretending things aren't falling apart when they are. There's a bright spot when watching your tiny humans grow and learn, and of course, those hugs and kisses are priceless. Sports mommin', birthday parties, milestone changes; slow down and take a moment, don't forget to clap for yourself. Reward yourself for surviving the days that you thought you wouldn't make it through.

> **NOBODY IS MORE FULL OF FALSE HOPE THAN A MOM WHO PLACES ITEMS ON THE STAIRS FOR FAMILY MEMBERS TO CARRY UP.**

Don't forget to take time for yourself. Don't forget that you too like sex, chocolate, wine, dates, trips, gifts, and lunch, as well as time *away* from your kids. Dress nicely for yourself some days, go to the store and apply the "NO" rule; if it's not for you, then it's a NO NO! Even if it's on sale (because we always say that). Give yourself a chore break; messy is okay, nasty is NOT!

Most importantly*** Learn to love yourself, including but not limited to; the way you look, walk and talk, your entire inner being, flaws and all. You're going to make mistakes, maybe you can't cook or clap on beat (side-eye) and it's okay, just breathe through it. Continue to invest in the things that bring you joy.

SHOW ME THE MONEY

Money, Money, Money, some, actually, many people have differing opinions on the topic of child support, but since this book is about single mothers, let's stay in that vein.

For us, it's the bare minimum that the state requires a man or woman, depending on custody, to pay. Putting your child's father on child support for many of us isn't our first desire, although many would have you believe that it is the only thing mothers want. Let me just say, umm, some of us use it as punishment; I'm not going to judge your pain because I do know it can be complicated.

My advice to you is that as you mature, find a way to have a conversation, especially if that's a sore spot between you and the child's father. Sometimes it is the only choice we are left with when they don't contribute or even tell you to put them on it because they feel like what you're asking for is too much.

Let's be very clear, the number the state calculates is more than likely not enough to cover all the child's expenses and needs, especially medical ugh. Every so often you will find someone that is forced to pay a crazy high amount because of the contrast in income.

Most of the time, all we mothers hear are complaints about paying; what we don't hear is anyone complaining about getting them up for school in the morning.

No complaints about dealing with their grumpiness, last-minute "I need a treat" or "have a project due today" requests, doing hair, or picky eating habits at six in the morning, before the day has even started.

We don't hear anyone complaining about the long a** car rider lines and fighting through traffic (while eating, doing makeup, making sure others don't oversleep) all of that and still trying to make it to work on time.

We don't hear no complaining about having to leave work because you got a call that he/she doesn't feel well and needs to be picked up from school/daycare, all while trying not to be mom-shamed by these male-dominated industries for having to leave when the kids need you because, after all, we are trying to climb the corporate ladder, heck any ladder for that matter that will allow us to make more money and advance our careers.

We don't hear no complaining when we don't have a personal life, private bathroom breaks, a moment of peace, food, or anything else to ourselves.

We sacrifice to make sure they have whatever they may need, sports equipment, shoes, clothes (sometimes they skip sizes ugh!), costumes and chile once they get into those grown-up sizes, the price doubles! As far as the subject of child support goes, use it for whatever you need to take care of for your kids, and yes don't be wasteful because some moms definitely are.

Those who pay don't get to dictate what our child needs or when they need it; they are judging from the stance of what they see. One month it might be you needing to pay for your utilities that you were short on because you spent extra money on something they needed the month before. The point is don't guilt trip yourself; take care of your kids and move on.

P.S. Fu*k that raggedy a** system that wants you to spend every free moment you have down there at the courts or DSS office begging for assistance, which will ultimately take them six months or more to get to you. The hours are always during the workday just like those damned doctors' appointments and who's going to pay you for those lost hours? Nobody! Bingo! So, listen, spend less time worried about what anybody else has to say and more time pouring into your children.

Chapter 3: Parenting Solo while Balancing Responsibilities

BREAK ME OFF A PIECE OF THAT VISITATION BAR

Now let's deal with visitation; Ladies, I understand firsthand ***thee*** struggle of disliking hell, possibly hating or being annoyed by the sight and sound of your baby's father, especially if the breakup was nasty; however, hear me out. No matter how petty, ugly, and horrible y'all fallout has or will become, do your best to make sure it doesn't interfere with your child having a relationship with both parents. If you don't think they are going to harm your children, let them spend time with him. If you believe they will, then do what you must; the law doesn't account for human error.

When I say that once y'all get on a regular schedule, you will be looking forward to those breaks, hunnnnyyy I mean that. The moment he cancels, you will be mad as hell about not getting your rest and relaxation. Working a regular job and working on your own career, while working on your mental health, while working on your friendships, while working on your relationship, while working on other personal goals, while trying to accommodate everyone else, while trying to sleep is exhausting. Trust me, sis... relax your mind. TAKE THE BREAK.

A good friend of mine once said: "Ain't nobody ever planned to just get by; never miss an opportunity to invest in yourself." Remember to give yourself credit for the small moments of sunshine that manage to show up in the midst of a monsoon.

Chapter 4: Emotional Well-being

"EW, THE DATING POOL HAS MARRIED PEOPLE IN IT…

Dating, well… dating is draining. Period. I want to personally say R.I.D.P. (Rest in dirty pussy) to all those men who know what you've been through and still choose to take you through it all over again. Some food for thought: we sometimes attract what we ourselves are (i.e., dating unavailable men because deep down inside you might not actually be ready or emotionally available). Date where you're going, not where you are. Think of yourself as worthy, not a liability; your children as a blessing, not as an obstacle to untangle. Date to enjoy yourself, not just to get married. If a man is married and telling you about all his problems, tell him to go handle his business and see you after. You need to see paperwork; don't even allow yourself the opportunity to get pulled into his life and emotions. It's hard to stop caring for someone once you become invested; you have no clue whether he's in or out of his marriage, the fact remains that you only know what he tells you. You want to be with a man that can make a decision because if he can't decide on something that affects his everyday life, what could he possibly add to yours? Marrying the wrong one is much worse than staying single. If you want something different, be willing to try something different. Hang in there, ladies, your Mr. Right is out there somewhere. He may be in a different color or size wrapper than you expected, so keep those toes done! If he's short that'll be the first thing he sees. I'm dying laughing because if he's tall I would love to say that your smile would be what he sees but I'm really thinking it'll be that dry scalp at the top of your head. Just kidding! Be careful who you allow around your kids and don't leave them alone with your suitors; too much is going on these days for young boys and girls.

Which leads me to the term Emotional Hustling; this is the only place in this book where there will be a man's perspective. A young man by the name of *David J Mack IV* introduced me to this term, and it blew my mind. The notion that people would keep you around to serve their own non-material needs and then have the audacity to make you feel bad about it. He gave of himself when he wrote this, and as I read it, the tears began to flow. I want to share it with you all because these are the words that so many of us desperately need to hear.

EMOTIONAL HUSTLING BY DAVID J MACK IV

In the dark recesses of the male psyche, rests the most dangerous type of person... the "emotional hustler." This is the man who uses his charm, charisma, and extroverted personality to keep women close but never commits to them. He spends time with women but won't sleep with them. He buys women nice gifts, but there is no earnest heart behind the gift. He actually listens to women and is very attentive, but he will never sacrifice for her. This is the man that checks most of the important relationship boxes, except true love. Emotional Hustling is the worst type of betrayal because it builds an unrealistic expectation and bond that will never be fulfilled. It leaves women feeling lied to, abandoned, and used. But even worse, it is hard to spot because it is often masked in charm, gifts, and socially celebrated traits.

What makes this even worse is that our society has never explored the dynamics of men who subconsciously "emotionally hustle" women... BUT are still respected because they don't cheat, lie or sleep around promiscuously. This is a very dangerous dichotomy because men can use the "nice guy" facade to be adored by the very women they hurt.

Using anyone for emotional purposes, including women, is a serious ethical issue that demands attention and reflection. Emotionally using women involves manipulating their feelings, trust, and vulnerability for personal gain, without genuine care or consideration for their well-being. This behavior is a form of emotional abuse and can have profound and lasting negative effects on the individuals involved. Let's explore the dynamics of emotionally using women, its impact, and the importance of fostering healthy, respectful relationships.

Emotional usage of women often manifests in various forms, including but not limited to manipulation, gaslighting, and exploitation of their empathy and nurturing qualities. It is essential to recognize that emotional manipulation can occur in different contexts, such as romantic relationships, friendships, or within the family dynamic. In romantic relationships, emotional usage of women may involve exploiting their affection, loyalty, and desire for intimacy. This can lead to a pattern of behavior where the individual seeks to satisfy their emotional needs without reciprocating or respecting the emotions of the woman involved.

The other side of emotional hustling is that men are rewarded for very low standards. Men are often rewarded if *they stay faithful, spend time with, and buy nice gifts for their female significant others. These are three very important traits, but they do not express love. Instead, they can reflect very superficial and low-frequency relationships. Family, social media, film, music, and pop culture amplify this sentiment because they highlight the men who have the resources to emotionally hustle women. Men with financial means are awarded for what they give to a female and not what they sacrifice for a female. This is the hustle. A smart emotionally hustling man is going to give unsuspecting women what society thinks they want... and not what they spiritually need.*

Furthermore, emotional usage of women can also be present in professional settings, where a woman's emotional labor is exploited without acknowledgment or compensation. This may occur when women are expected to provide emotional support, maintain harmony, and manage conflicts without due recognition or respect for their contributions. These dynamics contribute to a culture where women's emotions are devalued and exploited, perpetuating inequality and eroding trust.

Speaking of devalued emotions, one of my closest female friends absolutely hates the mantra and image of the "strong Black female." She argues that our culture perceives the iconic Black woman as being strong, but this image is actually a degrading sign of inferiority. It portrays Black women as the dumping ground for the world's problems. Only non-privileged Black women allow themselves to shoulder the pain of others. Black women have been put in this position because so many Black women have been raised without love. Black women are often taught love through loyalty and service to others.

For example: A good woman takes care of her man. A good woman is always there for her man. A good woman never leaves her man and is always there for her children. You can see how a woman's identity and worth are often defined through what they do for others. This is the breeding ground for women who fall prey to emotional hustling. So, it becomes very easy for men to emotionally hustle these types of women because "service" and "loyalty" are what emotionally manipulative males thrive upon.

The impact of emotionally using women is profound and can result in severe emotional distress, low self-esteem, and a diminished sense of self-worth. When individuals are emotionally used, they may experience feelings of betrayal, confusion, and a loss of trust in themselves and others. Over time, this can lead to anxiety, depression, and difficulties in forming healthy relationships in the future.

We see all of these traits expressed in too many women. The effects of emotional usage can extend beyond the individual, impacting their social interactions, professional life, and overall well-being.

To address the issue of emotionally using women, it is crucial to promote awareness, education, and the cultivation of healthy relationship dynamics. Empathy, respect, and open communication are essential components of nurturing respectful and mutually fulfilling relationships. Individuals must be encouraged to recognize and respect the emotional boundaries of others, fostering an environment where emotional manipulation is not tolerated or condoned.

In addition, promoting gender equality and challenging traditional gender roles can help combat the underlying societal factors that perpetuate emotional usage of women.

By advocating for equal rights, opportunities, and representation, we can work towards creating a more equitable society where individuals are valued for their intrinsic worth rather than being exploited for their emotional labor or vulnerabilities.

In conclusion, emotionally using women is a significant ethical concern that warrants attention and action. By recognizing the impact of emotional manipulation and fostering healthy relationship dynamics, we can work towards creating a society where individuals, regardless of gender, are respected, valued, and empowered to engage in relationships based on mutual trust, empathy, and genuine care. It is essential to promote awareness, education, and advocacy to address the root causes of emotional usage and create a culture of respect and equality.

The basis of true love is always vulnerability and sacrifice. Men have to actually give up something special or sacred to show love. A man with a lot of money is not showing love by buying gifts. A man with a lot of free time is not showing love by spending time with a woman. There is a deeper connection that can be actualized through sacrifice and vulnerability because true love is vulnerable. That is why they call it "falling" in love. There is no power or control. We just have to be careful, as a society, not to let superficial and surface-level traits take the place of real profound love. This is how you overcome the dangerous trappings of an emotional hustler.

Chapter 5: Empowering Your Children, Building Resilience, Fostering Independence

F* THEM KIDS (HA!)

Do you feel worthy of good things? Not just on holidays but in general. Do you take time out for your thoughts and feelings, unrelated to work and family needs?

Stop rescheduling joy, as the saying goes. Tomorrow didn't come for someone who thought it would this morning.

I can remember walking the bridge every day, teaching my kids not to call me during that time unless it was an emergency. Listening to music and walking is a great way to clear the mind and get a little exercise. Bedtime yoga easily found on YouTube is a whole vibe if that's your speed. Mental health is so important because stress is deadly and unhealthy. A lot of times we keep saying it'll go away; it's just temporary. The worst thought of all is thinking it's acceptable because "it comes with the job" of being a single parent. Wrong!

Don't become so comfortable with discomfort that it feels normal. Go get a massage, watch a movie, sip and paint, something that relaxes you. Some of us need to get back to our first love (not the man), the things that bring us joy. By the way, physical health is just as important as mental health. Instead of dieting, just make healthier choices one at a time, lifestyle changes. Small wins are still wins. Keep a food diary so you can see what you're putting in your body day to day. When you feel better, you tend to do better.

- Sitting in your car in the driveway eating food that you don't want to share with those little crumb snatchers IS self-care.

- Telling your kids to ask somebody else, anybody else, siblings, aunts and uncles, grandparents, etc. IS self-care.

- Not arguing with your kids about wearing clothes that don't match the season IS self-care.

- Forgiving yourself for providing what they need even though your heart wants to provide their needs and wants IS self-care.

- Going to the store and not buying them something every time they ask… you guessed it, self-care. As my friend would say, give yourself some grace.

New mothers, it's natural to feel like you're drowning and not doing "it" right, a note from us seasoned mothers: there's no such thing as mothering correctly; there's no manual, you have to get into your own rhythm. To my single mothers out here doing fabulous things, as I've said before, don't let the hard days win. Breaking the glass ceiling or climbing the broken ladder with the cracked first rung isn't easy and can sometimes leave bruises, cuts and scars that never heal. It can be a lonely road.

Sometimes it gets hard to process everything going on with all the background noise and distractions of life. Deep down inside, all you really want is just a break from all the constant pressure. You're not mad or angry about any one thing; you just want to catch a break, and you're hopeful that it will come sooner rather than later.

Chapter 6: Advocacy and Networking for Opportunities

GAME FACE ON...

I have talked a lot about what we go through and gave us a chance to vent, but now it's time to get down to business. How do we get past our biggest hurdles? Let's chat about it.

Finances are always a big one because most of us either don't make enough or make just enough to survive. There's always the option of taking a second job if you have help with your kids, not to mention the energy to actually work that job without getting fired for low performance. We sometimes fight against the guilt of having to be away from our children for such a long time; let's be honest, there's no happy medium here. The choices are between providing necessities or spending more time with them. I vote for more time with them while at the same time figuring out the best way to provide what they need.

    Working nights is an option if you have someone trustworthy to stay with them, but working hours that somewhat align with the school day or daycare hours are probably your best bet. Keep looking for jobs that have the potential for you to move up because that's the way you make more money. Knowing what the earnings threshold is for assistance if you receive it is important as well because trust me, I've been there where I made just a couple of hundred more than the limit and got cut off, which led me right back to the struggle bus. If you make $14/hr., for example, at your current job, look for one that pays $13/hr. and up with the potential to move up or the ability to get overtime at a higher rate; it gives you greater earning power over time. I know it's scary, but to get something you want, you have to be willing to do something different even when you're scared.

There were a lot of days when I felt like I wouldn't survive the hardships; you are going to have them too, but don't let go of hope. Stop avoiding bill collectors; it will only prolong your anguish. I know your anxiety shoots through the roof every time you see that 1-800 number calling. Fight that anxiety and take a deep breath, then answer the phone. Be honest about your ability to pay or not pay, for that matter. Ask them what options you have and make sure to honor any commitments you make. Don't promise them an amount that you KNOW you can't pay just because you're nervous. Reach out to community leaders, i.e., pastors, council members, representatives, principals, activists, etc., to see if there are any programs or resources in the area of help you need. Think outside the box; your car note, and insurance may be high, so think, does it have high mileage? Your state may offer a high mileage discount on taxes and insurance.

Do you work close by? It may be cheaper to use Uber or Lyft for a while to save money (especially if in danger of repo) until you can buy a cash car for a couple thousand dollars or so. Look for ways to cut down on your monthly bills as well; Google can help with ideas for this. A lot of churches and pantries offer food drives and giveaways; I've used them many times. They will help you stretch your meals; for instance, they might give you noodles, and now all you have to buy is sauce and meat for spaghetti, which is a fan favorite when it comes to meal stretching. There's a site called Gig Pro as well as others that will allow you to work for the day and get paid if you don't have time to commit to a second job completely.

Ladies, also, take your side hustle seriously; focus on developing it to make money and don't be shy about advertising it to those around you. You could possibly get a permit to vend food and sell something simple like hotdogs and chips at the local outlet or shopping center; again, this depends on the rules of your county. I'm just trying to get your creative juices flowing. The stress of not having enough resources to meet your needs can make you feel like you're drowning in depression with no way out. You may not want to get out of bed some days, FIGHT BACK! Talk to your doctor and be open about needing help for your emotional stability. There's no shame in that; I know because I've done it and felt embarrassed about admitting that I was struggling; you're not alone.

There are so many ways that children affect us; they make us happy, and sometimes they make us sad. They challenge us to be the best version of ourselves; they make us pay attention to the current world realities. They make us cry, but most of all, they make us human. They have no worries for the most part, besides waking up and going to school, same as we did once upon a time. It's not enough to want a miniature of yourself; you must want them to be better than you. This world is cold enough all on its own; do your best to be loving, understanding, supportive, and firm with them.

Kids need structure, love, and guidance; don't send them out into the world looking for what they should be getting and are longing for from home. You may not understand how important this is now, but as the old folks say, keep living… I'm sure one day that will change. Learn from them;

we know most of it, or so we think anyways, but sometimes we don't.

Let them see your struggle; also, let them see your victories. Teach them that trouble will come but that it doesn't last forever. As they get older and start "smelling" themselves, that mouth tends to get smart and attitude nasty and unbearable; have patience and discipline loaded up in the chamber because you'll need plenty of it. When you want to knock them out or cuss them out, have restraint because passing on toxicity won't bode well for any of, yawl. If you must send them to someone, pick someone you know and trust to give them guidance. Sometimes they just need to hear it from someone else; it doesn't mean you failed; there are just some things they will have to learn the hard way, and you have to let them. I was one of these teens, so I definitely got it back from my oldest daughter and I still have another who hasn't hit the teens yet. Lol. My boys have always been respectful for the most part, but if they ever decide to get out of line, TRUST, I'm still a 'G'! I also have enough male role models, mentors, and male family members that I can and will call in a hot minute, should I need to.

WHAT THE HEALTH?

Mom brain, memory loss, aches and pains, there are many lingering effects that come from pregnancy. The social and emotional effects of this are rarely talked about. After I had baby number five, I suffered severe short term memory loss, while it has never returned, I've learned how to work around and compensate for it by taking notes, and pictures and other things that help jog my memory.

I've tried some of the medicines and taking vitamins, but the only thing that ever really helped me was playing brain games. I was in shock because I thought there's no way just playing these games on my phone could help me.

The hormonal changes and chemical changes our bodies go through can be quite significant. Be encouraged you're not alone.

WHAT'S YOUR PLAN?

Coping with this life ain't easy; drinking, drugs, and anything else you are using to cope should be in moderation or not at all. If you need help but are ashamed, there are plenty of hotlines and helplines that you can call. No judgment. As we know, you can always call Jesus. Maybe you're not religious; that's fine. Sending up a prayer or two can't hurt. Meditating, mindfulness, yoga, Zumba, working out, walking, swimming, whatever you choose, just find something that soothes your soul and make time for it. If you don't make time to take care of yourself, you won't be able to take care of anyone else.

"P.S. If you're sleeping with or dating someone just to get help paying your bills, no judgment, just understand that this is NOT a long-term plan, and you should be thinking about your future as well as your kids, so if you haven't made a plan, do it NOW!

Don't sweat the small things and be very intentional about what you give your energy to. If your child's grades suck and you don't have it in you to know how or what to do, look for free tutors; social media and the school are good resources for this. If you do have bandwidth, volunteer, run for the school board, City Council, and other offices that affect the way you live and the environment around you and your kids. Decisions that control the quality of education, water, access to medical care, access to healthy foods, roads, etc. You can do anything you put your mind to; nobody knows it all, and the people currently in those spots are regular folks just like you. If you need a night off, look for places that offer a quick break like "Parent's night out" or church events where kids can go for a couple of hours; if friends and family have older kids, maybe pay them to babysit.

Teach your children to be (mostly) self-sufficient because that will take the pressure off of you. Buying kid-friendly containers for your house so that they can pour their own cereal and juice, meals they can prepare in the microwave or oven, vegetables with ranch, peanut butter and jelly sandwiches, meat sandwiches are all good ideas. I sometimes have a night called "everybody on your own," which is exactly as it sounds; I don't care if they eat cereal, sandwiches, fries, hot pockets, the choice is theirs.

Don't be afraid to go old school with activities; I do not recommend becoming your child's sole source of entertainment. They need to learn to entertain themselves; that will benefit you when you're tired and also teaches them to be independent. Take them to the park, tell them to play outside, have a movie night in the house, picnic, potlucks with family and friends again, just ideas. Perhaps you and a friend can trade babysitting nights; you watch hers one night and she watches yours another. More tools to add to your toolbox.

Get your rest; a lot of us function on a ¼ of a tank, and that's not good. Sleep is important. When you get a good night's rest, it improves your mood, brain performance, and keeps your heart healthy. It lowers blood sugar, reduces stress, lowers inflammation, and allows you to be energetic and alert. When you sleep, the brain and body slow down and recover. During sleep, your body reinforces your cardiovascular and immune systems and helps regulate your metabolism. If you have trouble sleeping, try melatonin; it's a natural sleep aid. I've also found that it helps with certain aches and pains. I'm not a doctor, I can only share my experiences with you because I don't take any of the "PM" over-the-counter medicines.

Digital parenting can be hard to keep up with, but there are some settings and sites that can help you keep up. Most apps such as Facebook, TikTok, YouTube, and Instagram have settings that will allow you to control what type of content your kids have access to. There are other sites such as www.esafety.gov.au, that will list sites and information you may not be familiar with. Don't be afraid to talk to your child's school about needing help understanding how to check their work or access things on their Chromebook.

Have those awkward, hard conversations with your kids; it's better that they get the information from someone who loves them and wants the best for them than in the streets or from other kids. You want them to have the know-how when they encounter different situations such as assessing what may seem harmless but may be a dangerous situation. I frequently ask my kids if they have had any problems with good touch and bad touch. Good touch can be a hug or a high five, bad touch is everything else that encompasses unwanted touching. I also teach them not to sit on anyone's lap, not to give out phone numbers and addresses over the internet to teens or other kids. According to statistics, most of the time, our kids are violated by someone they know. If this happens, alert the authorities IMMEDIATELY! EVEN if it's a loved one, you don't want this to happen to anyone else's child. Untreated trauma can show up in a multitude of ways, your child will need counseling, and so will you. Abuses of any kind aren't normal, and we should not be treating them as such.

Parenting is quite the rollercoaster, and parenting alone is a rollercoaster on speed! So, buckle up! And try to enjoy the ride. You're not crazy; yes, your kids lie, cry at the most inconvenient time, break stuff, hide stuff, misbehave, and when you ask who done it or what happened, they are not going to have any information about any of it!! LOL. Keep going, mommas!! It'll get better!

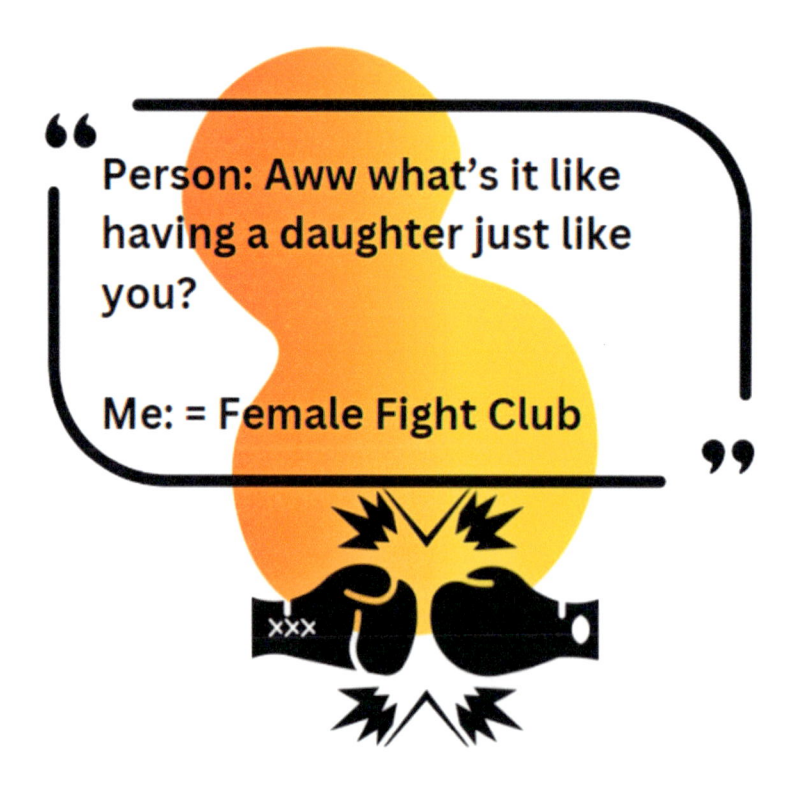

> "Person: Aww what's it like having a daughter just like you?
>
> Me: = Female Fight Club"

Chapter 7: Personal Achievements and Shaping a Positive Identity

HAVE A PLATE OF UNTREATED TRAUMA-

So many of us live with untreated trauma and pass it on to our kids. Recognizing those areas in yourself can help you identify when you're exhibiting those same traits when dealing with your kids. Co-parenting with the person you're healing from is not talked about enough. Working thru all those emotions and still having to deal with the person that triggers you should qualify us for an award. I'll give you another example; I was so mad at my teenage daughter one day, everything in me wanted to hit her in her disrespectful mouth, but at that very moment I had a flashback of when my father hit me in the head with a screwdriver. It was at that very moment I stopped myself and called her aunt to come and get her. Did she deserve to be popped in the mouth? I think so; however, the trauma that I went through and have had to, as an adult, working through something that happened so long ago wasn't anything that I wanted to pass on to my daughter and subsequently my grandkids and their kids and so on. Spanking is okay, but I was looking at an 18-year-old, not an 8-year-old. I made a conscious decision to not continue to pass on hurt.

Some would say that people who go through trauma are more likely to become something great, and it's because of those hardships they went through. I challenge you to have a different viewpoint. Hardships don't always have to be traumatic; challenging your children to be better doesn't have to be traumatic; teaching your children tenacity, follow through, perseverance, and self-confidence doesn't have to come through trauma.

What is trauma? Trauma is a lasting emotional response to a terrible event. Trauma most often affects our sense of self and often dictates the way we navigate relationships and the world around us.

When we allow the past to show up in our present, we invest so much time trying to work through it. Just think of how much further you could be in your life if you spent that same time and energy on your goals and dreams.

I know your pain and see your tears, the frustration and anger. I see it in the way you walk and talk; I see it in your eyes. I recognize that familiar feeling in the air of hoping for better and getting beat up every step along the way. I see the trauma of running back to the same broken relationships despite knowing they are no good for you, but the loneliness, the lonely nights, the lonely heartaches, it just creeps up on you, and how many of you know that creeping turns into wanting and longing. Listen here, don't let that temporary feeling send you back to the same trauma you left behind… That thing that was on your back is now under your feet! You're a conqueror, standing on the very thing that you thought would break you,

Standing on top of those who said you wouldn't be anything, said you weren't worth anything, said you would fail without them. Our trauma will not conquer us. Our latter will be greater, our children will be greater; this is our time! One of the reasons we are so exhausted is that we are oversaturated with information about the kind of parents we should be. So maybe it's time to stop reading the blogs that tell you how to raise the next president; perhaps it's time to embrace being the kind of parent who says sorry when you are wrong. Hugs them after a long day and makes peace with moment of chaos.

Chapter 8. The Conclusion of the matter

THE ART OF BEING MISUNDERSTOOD

If you spend your time waiting for people to go with you to your next level, you will become the queen of pump-faking! They are not on your timing; the purpose for your life isn't predicated on the vision or timing of others. It can be scary to go alone, but sometimes that's necessary. Being misunderstood will become an instant reality the moment you stop accepting behaviors from others that no longer serve your best interests. Not only will they not understand it, but they may not be ready to accept it. Interrupt negative thoughts: literally, you have to start filling those spaces with positive thoughts and affirmations instead. Affirmations are something you can write ahead of time and keep on a notecard or in your phone for those moments when you need a little boost, words of love and encouragement for yourself in moments of doubt. Hobbies are things you like to do purely for enjoyment; find them and don't feel the need to do anything with them, accept love it for what it is. Play your music and be in your space. Protect your mental health; stop hanging with people who dismiss your talents, who USED to be good to and for you, by setting solid boundaries. Don't make decisions based on the advice of those who don't have to live with the results. You are only one decision from a completely different life.

The reality is that you can be surrounded by lots of people and still feel alone. You are the driver of your sanity; it is determined by you. You must transition from nurturer to pusher as your children get older, and when you feel yourself reaching in relationships, be it family or friend, re-evaluate those connections.

You all are my motivation; I love to watch us win. This book goes out to all my baby mamas! You don't have to hate on the baby daddy to be a great baby mama, you don't have to be a TV housewife to be a great baby mama, all you have to do is keep being you!

Made in the USA
Columbia, SC
19 February 2024